ALL-AMERICAN
BARBECUE
COOKBOOK

BEEKMAN HOUSE

GRILLING FROM COAST TO COAST

Barbecue. Across the country the very word evokes emotions, tingles taste buds and rouses memories of summers gone by. It also creates controversy. Ask a few folks to define good barbecue and you're sure to ignite a raging debate. Some will even argue over the meaning of the word, contending *barbecue* means slow and *grilling* means fast over-the-coal cooking. This book has both methods.

The current barbecue craze started after World War II, but cooking out is one of America's oldest traditions, going back to the time when Indians slow-cooked their game over glowing coals. They adapted local ingredients for the open fire, smoking salmon over alder in the Northwest or roasting fruit-stuffed pigs in the South. However, it was the Caribbean natives who taught the Spanish to cook with a *barbacoa* or wooden frame and to baste meat with the spicy red mixtures that are most similar to today's barbecue sauces. The Spanish took these skills with them to the Southwest.

It was in the Southwest that ranchers, needing to feed hungry hired hands, adapted the barbacoa and spicy red sauces to barbecue whole sides of beef. Even today beef barbecue reigns in Texas. In the South, pork or pig pickin' is true barbecue. Along the coasts, the abundance of fish and seafood makes them popular grilling choices. And the Midwest offers an exciting variety of meats and sauces, from Kansas City beef and Iowa pork to German-style sausages. Turn the pages to discover more about grilling across the country, and if you want to know more about grilling techniques, turn to page 93.

QUALITY BARBECUE PRODUCTS

A big secret to the success of any cookout is using quality barbecue products from the Campbell family.

Zesty Open Pit barbecue sauce adds tang to recipes and makes an ideal basting sauce during cooking. Original Flavor Open Pit is available in 18-, 28- and 42-ounce sizes. For a change, try Hickory, Onion, Mesquite, Sweet or Hot flavors. And, if you prefer a thicker sauce, look for Thick & Tangy Open Pit in Original, Hickory and Mesquite flavors. Open Pit Special Recipe is even thicker and comes in Original, Hickory and Spicy flavors.

Sauces and glazes on grilled meats take on a silky smoothness when made with Franco-American Gravy. Look for Beef, Chicken, Mushroom, Turkey, Chicken Giblet, Au Jus and Pork Gravy or Brown Gravy with Onions.

No barbecue is complete without a pot of steaming baked beans. Campbell's Pork & Beans in Tomato Sauce works well in recipes and comes in 8-, 16-, 20¾-, 28- and 53-ounce sizes. You may find other flavors in your region too: Ranchero, Barbecue,

Home Style, Chili, Vegetarian and Old Fashioned Beans in Brown Sugar & Molasses Sauce.

Pickles and peppers make great barbecue condiments. Try Vlasic pickles, relishes, peppers and sauerkraut with sandwiches, salads or meats. Choose from Kosher, Polish, Zesty Dills, tangy Bread & Butter and lightly sweetened Country Classic Sweet Pickles in a variety of cuts and sizes. And for extra zip, turn to Vlasic mild or hot pepper rings or whole peppers. When a recipe calls for pickle or pepper juice, just use the juice from the jar.

Salads, made cool and creamy with Marie's Refrigerated Salad Dressings, round out any picnic menu. With tossed or layered salads, you'll enjoy trying a variety of Marie's Dressings: Blue Cheese, Buttermilk Spice, Ranch, Sour Cream and Dill, Italian Garlic, Italian Herb and Romano, Russian, Avocado Goddess, Classic Herb Vinaigrette, Red Wine Vinaigrette or Thousand Island. And, if you're counting calories, look for Lite Blue Cheese, Lite Sour Cream and Dill, Lite Italian Garlic and Lite Ranch dressings. Be sure to keep the salad dressings and dishes using them in the refrigerator.

Also making the salad or fresh vegetable scene is Campbell's Fresh line of produce: hydroponic or vine-ripened tomatoes, hydroponic butterhead lettuce and mushrooms. Mushrooms available are: Shiitake, oyster, classic brown "crimini" and common white (whole, sliced or gourmet stuffing size). Look for Campbell's Fresh produce and Marie's Dressings in your supermarket's produce section.

THE SOUTH

S ay "barbecue" in the South and you're immediately talking about pork. That's about all you can safely say because the sauces, pork cuts and cooking methods for true barbecue vary from state to state. Georgians like a sweet tomato sauce on their ribs. In Memphis, folks prefer pork sandwiches and vinegary sauce. In the Carolinas, pig pickin' means whole hog brushed with a mustard mop. However, one state to break the pork code is Kentucky, where mutton is popular. But, while Southerners argue over meat and sauce, they usually want the same foods served on the side: beans, coleslaw, biscuits and, in some parts, Brunswick Stew.

COUNTRY PICNIC

Menu serves 6

Sweet Georgia Barbecued Ribs

Spicy Lima Bean Bake

Southern-Style Slaw

Celery sticks

Radishes

Campbell's Fresh tomato wedges

Fluffy Biscuits

Watermelon or Plantation Pecan Pie

Lemonade

Sweet Georgia Barbecued Ribs, page 8; Spicy Lima Bean Bake, page 12; Southern-Style Slaw, page 14; Fluffy Biscuits, page 16; Plantation Pecan Pie, page 17

Pit-Style Pork Roast

Long, slow cooking over hickory chips is the secret behind a good Carolina pig pickin'.
And in Memphis, barbecue fans hanker for chopped barbecue pork sandwiches made
with a tangy red sauce.

Hickory chips
South Carolina Mustard Sauce or
Memphis Barbecue Sauce
(recipes follow)

5-pound pork shoulder blade
Boston roast

1. At least 1 hour before grilling, soak wood chips in enough water to cover. Drain wood chips. Prepare mustard sauce or barbecue sauce.

2. In covered grill, arrange preheated coals around drip pan; test for low heat above pan. Sprinkle 4 cups of the wood chips over coals. Insert a meat thermometer into thickest part of meat, without touching fat or bone.

3. On grill rack, place meat over pan but not over coals. Grill, covered, 3 hours or until well-done or 170°F. (allow 35 to 40 minutes per pound). Adjust vents and add charcoal and chips as needed. Brush with sauce the last hour. Makes 10 servings.

To roast: Place meat on rack in roasting pan. Roast, uncovered, at 325°F. 3 to 4 hours or until well-done or 170°F. (allow 40 to 45 minutes per pound). Brush often with sauce during the last hour.

Tennessee Pork Sandwiches: Shred cooked Pit-Style Pork Roast. Spoon pork onto 10 split and toasted hamburger buns. Top with coleslaw or Southern-Style Slaw (see recipe, page 14) and barbecue sauce. Makes 10 servings.

SOUTH CAROLINA MUSTARD SAUCE: In 1-quart saucepan, combine 1 cup cider vinegar, ½ cup prepared mustard, ⅓ cup sugar, 2 tablespoons seeded and finely chopped Vlasic hot chili peppers, 2 tablespoons butter or margarine, 2 teaspoons Worcestershire sauce, 1 teaspoon salt and 1 teaspoon chili powder. Over high heat, heat to boiling. Reduce heat to low; simmer, uncovered, 5 minutes, stirring often. Let stand at least 1 hour before using. Makes 2 cups.

MEMPHIS BARBECUE SAUCE: In 1-quart saucepan, combine 1 cup Open Pit original flavor barbecue sauce, ⅓ cup cider vinegar, 2 tablespoons butter or margarine and 2 tablespoons Worcestershire sauce. Heat to boiling. Reduce heat to low; simmer, uncovered, 5 minutes, stirring often. Makes about 1½ cups.

Cajun-Style Burgers

2 pounds ground beef
¼ cup seeded and chopped Vlasic
hot cherry peppers
½ teaspoon garlic powder
½ teaspoon onion powder
½ teaspoon black pepper

½ cup Open Pit original flavor
barbecue sauce
8 hamburger buns, split and
toasted
Vlasic zesty snack chunks

In large bowl, combine beef, cherry peppers, garlic, onion and black pepper. Shape into eight 1-inch-thick patties. On grill rack, place patties directly above medium coals. Grill, uncovered, until desired doneness (allow 10 minutes for medium and 12 minutes for well-done), turning and brushing often with barbecue sauce. Place patties on buns with snack chunks. Makes 8 servings.

Kentucky Barbecued Lamb

Folks in the sheep-farming region of southwestern Kentucky grill mutton slowly over a low fire, then slice or chop it for barbecue sandwiches.

Hickory chips
5-pound lamb leg roast
Black Dip (recipe follows)

Kentucky Barbecue Sauce
(recipe follows)

1. At least 1 hour before grilling, soak wood chips in enough water to cover. Drain wood chips.

2. In covered grill, arrange preheated coals around drip pan; test for low heat above pan. Sprinkle 4 cups of the wood chips over coals. Sprinkle lamb with salt. Insert a meat thermometer into thickest part of meat, without touching fat or bone.

3. On grill rack, place meat, fat side up, over pan but not over coals. Grill, covered, 3 hours or until medium or 160°F. (allow 30 to 35 minutes per pound). Adjust vents and add more charcoal and wood chips as necessary. Prepare Black Dip and Kentucky Barbecue Sauce. Brush meat with Black Dip every 30 minutes.

4. To serve: Let meat stand 15 minutes; thinly slice across the grain. Serve with Kentucky Barbecue Sauce. Makes 12 servings.

To roast: Place meat, fat side up, on rack in roasting pan. Roast, uncovered, at 325°F. 1½ to 3 hours or until desired doneness (allow 20 to 25 minutes per pound for rare or 140°F., 25 to 30 minutes per pound for medium or 160°F. and 30 to 35 minutes per pound for well-done or 170°F.). Brush with Black Dip every 30 minutes.

Kentucky Lamb Sandwiches: Slice cooked Kentucky Barbecued Lamb; place on 12 split and toasted hamburger buns. Top with sliced onions and Vlasic original hamburger dill chips. Spoon on Kentucky Barbecue Sauce. Makes 12 servings.

BLACK DIP: In 1-quart saucepan, combine 1 cup vinegar, ½ cup water, ¼ cup Worcestershire sauce, 1½ teaspoons lemon juice and ¼ teaspoon pepper. Over high heat, heat to boiling. Makes 1¾ cups.

KENTUCKY BARBECUE SAUCE: In 1-quart saucepan, combine 1 cup Open Pit original flavor barbecue sauce, 1 cup tomato puree and 1 tablespoon butter or margarine. Over medium heat, heat through, stirring until butter is melted. Serve warm. Makes 2 cups.

If you like smoke-flavored meats, sprinkle damp wood chips over hot coals and cover to retain the smoke. Recipes in this book specify hickory or mesquite chips, which are commonly available. You may want to try other regional hardwoods such as oak, pecan, walnut, apple, cherry, peach, pear, Osage orange, alder, maple or grapevine. (Do not use pine or other resinous woods.) Remember to soak wood chips before grilling, so they'll smolder, not burn.

Sweet Georgia Barbecued Ribs

Georgians often serve barbecued ribs between two slices of bread . . . bones and all. They coat the slabs with either a thin hot sauce or a sweet tomato sauce, like the one below. Pictured on page 5.

1 bottle (18 ounces) Open Pit **original flavor barbecue sauce**	**¼ cup Worcestershire sauce**
¾ cup packed brown sugar	**3 tablespoons butter or margarine**
⅓ cup cider vinegar	**2 tablespoons dry mustard**
	6 pounds pork spareribs (2 slabs)

1. To make sauce: In 2-quart saucepan, combine barbecue sauce, sugar, vinegar, Worcestershire, butter and mustard. Over high heat, heat to boiling. Reduce heat to low; simmer, uncovered, 5 minutes, stirring often. Let stand at least 1 hour before using.

2. In covered grill, arrange preheated coals around drip pan; test for medium heat above pan. On grill rack, place ribs, fat side up, over pan but not over coals. Grill, covered, 1½ to 2 hours or until well-done. Adjust vents and add more charcoal as necessary. Turn and brush with sauce every 30 minutes. Makes 6 servings.

To roast: Place ribs, fat side up, on rack in pan. Roast, uncovered, at 350°F. 1½ to 2 hours or until well-done. Turn; brush with sauce every 30 minutes.

Brunswick Stew

Brunswick Stew has evolved from squirrel soup. Pictured opposite.

5-pound stewing chicken, cut up	**1 can (16 ounces) whole tomatoes,** **undrained, cut up**
6 cups water	
2 bay leaves	**1 can (8 ounces) whole kernel** **golden corn, drained**
2 teaspoons salt	
½ teaspoon pepper	**1 cup frozen lima beans**
4 slices bacon, cut into ½-inch **pieces**	**1 tablespoon Worcestershire** **sauce**
2 medium onions, sliced and **separated into rings**	**1 can (20 ounces) Campbell's pork** **& beans in tomato sauce**
2 medium potatoes, peeled and **cubed**	**2 tablespoons chopped fresh** **parsley (optional)**

1. In 6-quart Dutch oven, combine chicken, 6 cups water, bay leaves, salt and pepper. Over high heat, heat to boiling. Reduce heat to low; simmer, covered 2½ hours or until tender.

2. Strain broth; skim fat. Reserve 4 cups broth (add water to equal 4 cups). Discard bay leaves. When cool, remove chicken from bones; cut up chicken.

3. In same Dutch oven, cook bacon until crisp. Drain on paper towels. Spoon off all but 2 tablespoons drippings. Add onions; cook until tender, stirring often. Stir in potatoes, tomatoes, corn, lima beans, Worcestershire, reserved broth and chicken. Heat to boiling. Reduce heat; simmer, uncovered, 30 minutes. Stir in pork & beans. Simmer, uncovered, 30 minutes longer. Stir in bacon. Add parsley, if desired. Makes 12 cups or 12 servings.

Brunswick Stew

Blackened Chicken

To capture the essence of open-fire cooking, New Orleans chef Paul Prudhomme began blackening foods in an extremely hot iron skillet. Using similar seasonings, this chicken version "blackens" over hot coals. For even more zip, increase black pepper to ½ teaspoon. Pictured opposite.

½ teaspoon salt
½ teaspoon garlic powder
½ teaspoon paprika
¼ teaspoon onion powder
¼ teaspoon black pepper
¼ teaspoon ground cumin
3 whole chicken breasts, split, skinned and boned (1½ pounds boneless)

2 tablespoons seeded and chopped Vlasic hot chili or jalapeno peppers
¼ cup butter or margarine
Plum tomato slices for garnish
Snipped fresh parsley for garnish

1. In small bowl, combine salt, garlic, paprika, onion, black pepper and cumin.

2. With meat mallet or rolling pin, pound chicken breasts to ¼-inch thickness. Rub hot chili peppers evenly over one side of each breast half. In 8-inch skillet over low heat, melt butter. Dip chicken into butter. Rub seasoning mixture evenly over both sides of chicken. Reserve remaining butter.

3. On grill rack, place chicken directly above hot coals. Drizzle 1 teaspoon reserved butter over each piece of chicken. (Be careful as the fire will flare up.) Grill, uncovered, 3 minutes. Turn chicken. Drizzle with remaining butter. Grill 2 minutes more or until tender and juices run clear. Garnish with tomato and parsley. Makes 6 servings.

Honey-Lemon Chicken

A Southern Sunday supper often means fried chicken and gravy. Here's a grilled chicken-and-gravy dish, lightly accented with honey and lemon.

1 can (10½ ounces) Franco-American chicken gravy
2 tablespoons honey
½ teaspoon grated lemon peel

1 tablespoon lemon juice
2½- to 3-pound broiler-fryer chicken, cut up

1. To make sauce: In 1-quart saucepan, combine gravy, honey, peel and juice. Over medium-high heat, heat to boiling, stirring constantly.

2. On grill rack, place chicken, skin side up, directly above medium coals. Grill, uncovered, 1 hour or until tender and juices run clear, turning and brushing often with sauce during the last 30 minutes. Makes 6 servings.

To broil: Arrange chicken, skin side up, on rack in broiler pan. Broil 6 inches from heat 40 minutes or until tender and juices run clear, turning and brushing often with sauce during the last 20 minutes.

Blackened Chicken

Cajun-Style Beans

Classic Louisiana Cajun ingredients—onions, celery, peppers and garlic—flavor this hot bean side dish. Pictured opposite and on front cover.

1 tablespoon butter or margarine
½ cup diced cooked ham
½ cup chopped onion
1 stalk celery, chopped
1 medium green pepper, chopped
1 large clove garlic, minced

1 can (16 ounces) Campbell's pork & beans in tomato sauce
2 tablespoons chopped pimento
¼ teaspoon black pepper
⅛ teaspoon ground red pepper

In 10-inch skillet over medium heat, in hot butter, cook ham, onion, celery, green pepper and garlic until vegetables are tender, stirring often. Stir in beans, pimento, black pepper and red pepper. Over high heat, heat to boiling. Reduce heat to low; simmer, uncovered, 5 minutes, stirring occasionally. Makes 3 cups or 6 servings.

Beans with Pineapple

Grill a center slice of ham to serve alongside these beans.

1 can (28 ounces) Campbell's pork & beans in tomato sauce
¼ cup molasses

1 can (8 ounces) pineapple chunks in juice, drained

In 10-inch skillet, combine beans and molasses; heat to boiling. Add pineapple chunks; heat through. Makes 3 cups or 6 servings.

Spicy Lima Bean Bake

This bean dish gets a flavor boost from bacon instead of the old fashioned salt pork. Pictured on page 5.

4 slices bacon, quartered
1 small onion, sliced and separated into rings
1 teaspoon chili powder
1 can (16 ounces) Campbell's pork & beans in tomato sauce

1 package (10 ounces) frozen baby lima beans, cooked and drained
½ cup Open Pit original flavor barbecue sauce

1. In 10-inch skillet over medium heat, cook bacon until crisp. Transfer to paper towels to drain. Spoon off all but 1 tablespoon drippings. In hot drippings, cook onion and chili powder 5 minutes or until onion is tender, stirring often. Stir in beans and barbecue sauce.

2. Transfer mixture to 1-quart casserole; top with bacon. Bake, uncovered, at 350°F. 30 minutes or until most of sauce is absorbed. Stir before serving. Makes 3½ cups or 6 servings.

Cajun-Style Beans

Louisiana-Style Potato Salad

This Louisiana twist on potato salad includes a dash of hot sauce. Pictured opposite.

**2 pounds small new potatoes,
 sliced ¼ inch thick (6 cups)**
**5 slices bacon, cut into ½-inch
 pieces**
**¾ cup Marie's refrigerated sour
 cream and dill salad dressing**
**1 to 2 tablespoons Louisiana-style
 hot sauce**

¼ teaspoon black pepper
1 medium green pepper, diced
½ cup sliced green onions
**½ cup chopped Vlasic original dill
 pickles**
**Campbell's Fresh butterhead
 lettuce leaves**

1. In 4-quart saucepan over medium heat, cook potatoes in boiling water to cover 10 minutes or until tender. Drain.

2. In 8-inch skillet over medium heat, cook bacon until crisp. Transfer to paper towels to drain. Reserve 1 tablespoon bacon drippings.

3. In small bowl, combine salad dressing, hot sauce, black pepper, bacon and reserved drippings. In large bowl, combine potatoes, green pepper, onions and pickles. Add dressing mixture; toss to coat. Cover; refrigerate at least 4 hours. Serve in lettuce-lined salad bowl. Makes 8 cups or 8 servings.

Southern-Style Slaw

Southerners love their slaw in barbecue sandwiches. Pictured on page 5.

**1 cup Marie's refrigerated
 buttermilk spice ranch style
 salad dressing**
3 tablespoons cider vinegar
2 tablespoons sugar

1 teaspoon prepared mustard
¼ teaspoon celery seed
¼ teaspoon pepper
6 cups shredded cabbage
1 cup shredded carrots

In medium bowl, combine salad dressing, vinegar, sugar, mustard, celery seed and pepper. Add cabbage and carrots; toss gently to coat. Cover; refrigerate until serving time, at least 2 hours. Makes 5½ cups or 6 servings.

Fried Pickles

Fried pickles frequently co-star with fried catfish in the Mississippi Delta.

Vegetable oil for deep-fat frying
1¼ cups all-purpose flour, divided
1 teaspoon black pepper
½ teaspoon ground red pepper

1 cup beer
**1 jar (16 ounces) Vlasic zesty or
 Polish snack chunks, drained**

In 5-quart Dutch oven, heat 1½ inches oil to 375°F. In medium bowl, stir together ¾ cup of the flour and peppers; stir in beer. In small bowl, place remaining ½ cup flour. Coat snack chunks in flour, then dip into beer batter. Fry snack chunks, a few at a time, in hot oil 2 minutes or until golden brown on both sides. Transfer to paper towels to drain. Makes about 80 appetizers.

Louisiana-Style Potato Salad

Fluffy Biscuits

Serve these Old South favorites freshly baked and butter-melting hot. Pictured on page 5.

2 cups all-purpose flour	**½ cup shortening**
1 tablespoon baking powder	**¾ cup milk**
¼ teaspoon salt	

1. Preheat oven to 450°F. In large bowl, stir together flour, baking powder and salt. With pastry blender or fork, cut in shortening until mixture resembles coarse crumbs. Add milk. With fork, mix just until mixture forms a soft dough that leaves sides of bowl.

2. Turn dough onto lightly floured surface; knead 6 to 8 strokes until mixed. Roll out to ½-inch thickness. With floured 2½-inch biscuit cutter, cut into rounds, using straight downward motion (do not twist).

3. Place biscuits on ungreased cookie sheet about 1 inch apart. Bake 10 minutes or until golden. Makes 12 biscuits.

Bourbon Street Chocolate Bread Pudding

Chocolate jazzes up this New Orleans French Quarter favorite.

1½ cups milk	**2 tablespoons bourbon**
½ cup semi-sweet chocolate pieces	**2 cups cubed day-old French bread**
3 eggs	**Whipped cream**
⅓ cup sugar	

1. In 1-quart saucepan over low heat, heat milk and chocolate pieces until milk is warm and chocolate pieces are softened, stirring occasionally.

2. In large bowl, beat eggs. Stir in warm milk mixture, sugar and bourbon. Place bread cubes in 1-quart casserole. Pour milk mixture over bread; stir gently to coat.

3. Place large shallow baking pan on middle rack of oven. Carefully place casserole with mixture into baking pan. Fill baking pan with hot water to depth of 1 inch. Bake, uncovered, at 350°F. 45 minutes or until knife inserted in center comes out clean. Serve warm or chilled with whipped cream. Makes 6 servings.

Plantation Pecan Pie

With pecan trees all around them, Southerners have a natural affinity for anything made with the nuts, especially pie. Pictured on page 5.

3 eggs	¼ cup butter or margarine, melted
1 cup dark corn syrup or cane syrup	1 teaspoon vanilla extract
	1½ cups pecan halves
½ cup sugar	9-inch unbaked pie crust

1. Preheat oven to 350°F. In large bowl, beat eggs. Stir in syrup, sugar, butter and vanilla. Stir in pecans. Pour into crust.

2. Bake, uncovered, 35 to 40 minutes or until knife inserted about 1½ inches from edge comes out clean. Cool on wire rack. Makes 8 servings.

Double Lime Soufflé

Popular along the West and Florida Coasts, tangy, tropical lime makes a refreshing dessert ingredient.

2 envelopes unflavored gelatin	⅛ teaspoon green or yellow food coloring (optional)
¾ cup sugar, divided	
8 eggs, separated	2 cups heavy or whipping cream
1 cup lime or lemon juice	Lime or lemon slices for garnish
⅔ cup cold water	
1 teaspoon grated lime peel or 2 teaspoons grated lemon peel	

1. In double-boiler top, combine gelatin and ¼ cup of the sugar. In small bowl, beat egg yolks, juice and cold water until mixed; stir into gelatin mixture. Place over double-boiler bottom containing hot, not boiling, water. Cook until mixture thickens slightly and coats metal spoon, stirring constantly. Remove from heat; stir in peel and food coloring. Pour into large bowl; cool to room temperature, stirring occasionally.

2. Measure 12-inch-wide strip of foil to fit around 2-quart soufflé dish; fold in half. Carefully wrap foil strip around outside of dish so collar stands about 3 inches above rim. Fasten securely with tape.

3. In small bowl with mixer at high speed, beat egg whites until soft peaks form; gradually beat in remaining ½ cup sugar until stiff peaks form. In small bowl with mixer at medium speed, whip cream. Gently fold beaten egg whites and whipped cream into cooled gelatin mixture. Turn into prepared soufflé dish. Cover; refrigerate until set, at least 6 hours.

4. To serve: Carefully remove foil collar; garnish with citrus slices. Makes 10 servings.

— THE SOUTHWEST —

Southwest-style barbecue evolved on the dusty cow trail, where saddle-weary ranch hands needed lots of food with lots of flavor. They chowed down on barbecued beef, beans, corn bread and foods from the region's Indian-Spanish heritage. Barbecued beef is still the law of the land, particularly in Texas where brisket is popular. Today, the Pueblo Indian, Spanish and Mexican influences are more visible than ever. Indian dishes such as beans, tortillas and corn bread frequently appear on barbecue tables. Peppers of all kinds add heat to sauces and side dishes. And the Spanish legacy offers some intriguing spice combinations and rich desserts.

RANCH BARBECUE

Menu serves 15

Nachos

Texas Beef Brisket

Barbecue Beans

Campbell's Fresh
tomato wedges

Endive

Avocado slices

Cheesy Pepper
Corn Bread

Fresh fruit or Mexican
Wedding Cookies

Coffee

Texas Beef Brisket, page 20; Barbecue Beans, page 31; Cheesy Pepper Corn Bread, page 35; Mexican Wedding Cookies, page 35

Texas Beef Brisket

Texans will argue whether sauce should be brushed onto the meat during grilling or served along with the meat at the table. Sauce aside, they do agree that brisket needs long, slow cooking to be juicy and tender. Pictured on page 19.

1½ cups Open Pit original flavor
    barbecue sauce
⅓ cup Worcestershire sauce
⅓ cup molasses or dark corn syrup
½ teaspoon garlic powder
½ teaspoon onion powder

5- to 6-pound beef brisket
Avocado slices for garnish
Campbell's Fresh tomato
    wedges for garnish
Curly endive for garnish

1. To make sauce: In medium bowl, combine barbecue sauce, Worcestershire, molasses, garlic and onion.

2. In covered grill, arrange preheated coals around drip pan; test for low heat above pan. On grill rack, place meat over pan but not over coals. Grill, covered, 2½ to 3 hours or until tender (allow 30 minutes per pound). Adjust vents and add more charcoal as necessary. Turn and brush often with sauce during the last hour.

3. To serve: Thinly slice meat across grain. Garnish with avocado, tomato and endive. Heat remaining sauce; serve with meat. Makes 15 servings.

To roast: Place meat, fat side up, on rack in roasting pan. Roast, uncovered, at 325°F. 2 to 3 hours or until tender (allow 30 minutes per pound). Turn and brush often with sauce during the last hour.

Chili-Rubbed Brisket

Texas barbecue experts swear this traditional spice-rubbed brisket will be moister if you leave the fat on and turn the meat with tongs, instead of a fork.

5- to 6-pound beef brisket or chuck
    blade roast
2 tablespoons chili powder
1 tablespoon sugar
1 tablespoon garlic powder

1 tablespoon seasoned salt or
    hickory smoked salt
2 teaspoons paprika
1 teaspoon ground red pepper
Mesquite or hickory chips

1. Place meat in large shallow nonmetal dish. In small bowl, combine chili powder, sugar, garlic, salt, paprika and pepper; rub over meat. Cover; refrigerate at least 4 hours or overnight.

2. At least 1 hour before grilling, soak wood chips in enough water to cover. Drain wood chips.

3. In covered grill, arrange preheated coals to one side of grill, away from pan. Test for low heat above pan. Sprinkle 4 cups of the wood chips over coals.

4. On grill rack, place meat over pan but not over coals. Grill, covered, 2½ to 3 hours or until tender (allow 30 minutes per pound). Adjust vents; add charcoal and wood chips as necessary.

5. To serve: Thinly slice meat across grain. Makes 15 servings.

To roast: Place meat, fat side up, on rack in roasting pan. Roast, uncovered, at 325°F. 2 to 3 hours or until tender (allow 30 minutes per pound), turning once.

Rib Eye Steak with Red Pepper Gravy

1 large sweet red or yellow pepper
6 beef rib eye steaks, cut 1 inch
   thick
1 can (10¼ ounces) Franco-
   American beef gravy
½ teaspoon garlic powder
¼ teaspoon ground red pepper
¼ cup whole kernel corn, cooked
2 tablespoons butter or margarine

1. To roast pepper: On grill rack, place pepper directly above medium coals. Grill, uncovered, 10 to 15 minutes or until blistered and charred, turning occasionally. Place in paper bag; let steam 5 minutes.

2. On grill rack, place steaks directly above medium coals. Grill, uncovered, until desired doneness (allow 15 minutes for rare and 20 minutes for medium), turning once during cooking.

3. To make gravy: Peel and halve pepper; remove seeds. In covered blender or food processor, blend until smooth. In 1-quart saucepan, combine pepper puree, gravy, garlic and red pepper. Over medium-high heat, heat to boiling, stirring constantly. Reduce heat to low; simmer, uncovered, 10 minutes, stirring occasionally. Stir in corn and butter; heat until butter is melted. Serve gravy with steaks. Makes 6 servings.

To broil: Arrange steaks on rack in broiler pan. Broil 4 inches from heat until desired doneness (allow 15 minutes for rare and 20 minutes for medium), turning once during cooking.

Hot 'n' Spicy Cheese Burgers

Team these peppery burgers with a Vlasic zesty dill spear.

1½ pounds ground beef
¼ cup seeded and chopped Vlasic
   hot banana peppers
½ teaspoon ground cumin
½ cup Open Pit original flavor
   barbecue sauce
6 thin slices Cheddar cheese
6 onion or hamburger buns, split
   and toasted

1. In large bowl, combine beef, peppers and cumin. Shape into six 1-inch-thick patties.

2. On grill rack, place patties directly above medium coals. Grill, uncovered, until desired doneness (allow 10 minutes for medium and 12 minutes for well-done), turning and brushing often with barbecue sauce. The last minute of grilling, top with cheese slices; heat until melted.

3. To serve: Place patties on buns. Makes 6 servings.

To broil: Arrange patties on rack in broiler pan. Broil 4 inches from heat until desired doneness (allow 15 minutes for medium and 18 minutes for well-done), turning and brushing often with barbecue sauce. The last minute of broiling, top with cheese slices; heat until melted.

Grilled Flank Steak with Southwest Sauce

Serve any remaining sauce over hamburgers or steak. Pictured opposite.

½ cup Burgundy or other dry red
  wine
¼ cup vegetable oil
2 cloves garlic, minced and divided
1½-pound beef flank steak
⅓ cup chopped onion
1 can (16 ounces) stewed
  tomatoes, undrained
¾ cup Open Pit original flavor
  barbecue sauce
1 to 2 tablespoons seeded and
  chopped Vlasic hot jalapeno
  peppers

½ teaspoon dried oregano leaves,
  crushed
½ teaspoon ground cumin
¼ teaspoon ground coriander
  Sweet red pepper rings for
  garnish
  Vlasic hot jalapeno peppers for
  garnish
  Fresh cilantro for garnish

1. To marinate: In large shallow nonmetal dish, combine wine, oil and 1 clove garlic. Add steak; turn to coat. Cover; refrigerate at least 4 hours or overnight, turning occasionally. Drain steak, reserving ¼ cup of the marinade.

2. To make sauce: In 2-quart saucepan over medium-high heat, heat reserved marinade to boiling. Add remaining garlic and onion; cook until tender, stirring often. Stir in tomatoes, barbecue sauce, chopped peppers, oregano, cumin and coriander; heat to boiling. Reduce heat; simmer, uncovered, 15 minutes or until reduced to 2 cups, stirring occasionally.

3. On grill rack, place meat directly above medium-hot coals. Grill, uncovered, until desired doneness (allow 10 minutes for rare and 14 minutes for medium), turning once.

4. To serve: Thinly slice meat across grain. Garnish with pepper rings, jalapeno peppers and cilantro. Serve with sauce. Makes 6 servings.

To broil: Place meat on rack in broiler pan. Broil 4 inches from heat until desired doneness (allow 10 minutes for rare and 12 minutes for medium), turning once.

Barbecue Beef Sandwiches

Here's brisket in a bun smothered with zesty barbecue sauce—a Southwest treat. See page 20 for directions on cooking beef brisket.

1 pound chopped smoked beef
  brisket or cooked beef
¾ cup Open Pit original flavor
  barbecue sauce

1 tablespoon packed brown sugar
4 hamburger buns, split and
  toasted
  Vlasic sweet salad cubes

In 2-quart saucepan, combine meat, barbecue sauce and sugar. Over medium heat, heat to boiling. Reduce heat to low; simmer, covered, 25 minutes, stirring often. Serve in buns with salad cubes. Makes 4 servings.

Grilled Flank Steak with Southwest Sauce

Fast Chili

Chili purists debate using tomatoes and beans in "bowls of red." This version uses both. In the Southwest, cooks may also use a coarse chili grind for the meat, but ground beef makes a good substitute. Top with your choice of Vlasic cherry peppers, cheese, sour cream, olives or green onion. Pictured opposite.

1 pound chili grind or ground beef
1 cup chopped onions
2 large cloves garlic, minced
1 tablespoon chili powder
1 can (8 ounces) tomatoes,
    undrained, cut up
¼ cup Open Pit original flavor
    barbecue sauce

1 can (28 ounces) Campbell's pork
    & beans in tomato sauce or
    2 cans (15½ ounces *each***)**
    Campbell's Ranchero beans
2 tablespoons seeded and
    chopped Vlasic mild cherry
    peppers
Corn bread or hot cooked rice

1. In 10-inch skillet over medium-high heat, cook beef, onions, garlic and chili powder until beef is browned and onions are tender, stirring to separate meat. Spoon off fat.

2. Stir in tomatoes and barbecue sauce; cook 1 minute. Stir in beans; heat to boiling. Reduce heat to low; simmer, uncovered, 10 minutes, stirring occasionally. Stir in peppers.

3. To serve: Spoon over corn bread or rice. Makes 6 cups or 6 servings.

To microwave: In 2-quart microwave-safe casserole, combine beef, onions, garlic and chili powder. Microwave, covered, on HIGH 5 minutes or until no pink remains in meat, stirring once. Spoon off fat. Stir in tomatoes, barbecue sauce and beans. Microwave, covered, on HIGH 7 minutes or until heated through, stirring twice. Stir in peppers.

Glazed Smoked Sausage

If you can't find the hot link sausage served in the German towns of the Texas hill country, substitute kielbasa or Polish sausage.

⅓ cup Open Pit original flavor
    barbecue sauce
¼ cup packed brown sugar

3 tablespoons cider vinegar
1 pound cooked smoked sausage
    (kielbasa)

1. To make glaze: In small bowl, combine barbecue sauce, sugar and vinegar.

2. Score sausage diagonally. On grill rack, place sausage directly above medium coals. Grill, uncovered, 20 minutes or until hot, turning and brushing often with glaze. Makes 4 main-dish or 16 appetizer servings.

To broil: Place sausage on rack in broiler pan. Broil 4 inches from heat 15 minutes or until hot, turning and brushing often with glaze.

Fast Chili

Sweet Jalapeno Ribs

You'll find jalapeno jelly in the Mexican or condiment section of your grocery store. Serve leftover jelly with cream cheese and crackers. Pictured on front cover.

1½ cups Open Pit original flavor barbecue sauce
½ cup jalapeno jelly
¼ cup cider vinegar

2 tablespoons seeded and chopped Vlasic hot jalapeno peppers
2 teaspoons garlic powder
6 pounds pork spareribs (2 slabs)

1. To make sauce: In 1-quart saucepan, combine barbecue sauce, jelly, vinegar, peppers and garlic. Over medium heat, heat until jelly melts, stirring often.

2. In covered grill, arrange preheated coals around drip pan; test for medium heat above pan. On grill rack, place ribs, fat side up, over pan but not over coals. Grill, covered, 1½ to 2 hours or until well-done. Adjust vents; add more charcoal as necessary. Turn; brush often with sauce during the last 30 minutes. Makes 6 servings.

To roast: Place ribs, fat side up, on rack in roasting pan. Roast, uncovered, at 350°F. 1½ to 2 hours or until well-done. Turn and brush often with sauce during the last 30 minutes.

Beefy Bean Tacos

Tacos show how the Pueblo Indian and Spanish cuisines have blended in the Southwest. Spanish beef and onions plus Indian corn and beans.

½ pound ground beef
½ cup chopped onion
1 tablespoon chili powder
1 can (16 ounces) Campbell's pork & beans in tomato sauce or 1 can (15½ ounces) Campbell's Ranchero beans
¼ cup seeded and chopped Vlasic mild or hot banana peppers

10 taco shells
Shredded lettuce
Diced Campbell's Fresh tomatoes
Vlasic mild or hot banana pepper rings
Shredded sharp Cheddar cheese

1. In 10-inch skillet over medium-high heat, cook beef, onion and chili powder until beef is browned and onion is tender, stirring to separate meat. Spoon off fat.

2. Stir in beans and chopped peppers, pressing with spoon to mash beans. Cook, uncovered, 5 minutes or until thick, stirring occasionally.

3. To serve: Spoon about ¼ cup bean mixture into each taco shell. Top with lettuce, tomatoes, pepper rings and cheese. Makes 10 tacos or 5 servings.

To microwave: In 1-quart microwave-safe casserole, combine beef, onion and chili powder. Microwave, covered, on HIGH 3 minutes or until no pink remains in meat, stirring once. Spoon off fat. Stir in beans and chopped peppers. Microwave, covered, on HIGH 3 minutes or until heated through, stirring once.

Beefy Bean Tostadas: Prepare as above, except spread ¼ cup bean mixture on each of 10 tostada shells. Top with lettuce, tomatoes, pepper rings and cheese.

Spiced Mixed Meat Kabobs

It's not uncommon to see two or three meat dishes at a Southwestern barbecue. Here's a way to serve a combination on a kabob.

½ cup Open Pit original flavor
    barbecue sauce
½ teaspoon grated orange peel
2 tablespoons orange juice
2 tablespoons vegetable oil
1 tablespoon packed brown sugar
¼ teaspoon ground cinnamon

1 whole chicken breast, split,
    skinned, boned and cut into
    strips (½ pound boneless)
½ pound boneless pork tenderloin,
    cut into 1-inch pieces
½ pound boneless beef sirloin, cut
    into ¾-inch pieces

1. To marinate: In large shallow nonmetal dish, combine barbecue sauce, peel, juice, oil, sugar and cinnamon. Add chicken, pork and beef pieces; stir to coat. Cover; refrigerate 4 hours, stirring occasionally.

2. Drain meats, reserving marinade. On 6 metal skewers, alternately thread meats. On grill rack, place kabobs directly above hot coals. Grill, uncovered, 10 minutes or until chicken and pork are well-done, turning and brushing often with marinade. Makes 6 servings.

To broil: Arrange kabobs on rack in broiler pan. Broil 4 inches from heat 10 minutes or until well-done, turning and brushing often with marinade.

Tequila-Orange Chicken

Though traditionally served in shot glasses with limes and salt, tequila acts as a flavor accent in Southwest cooking too.

½ cup orange juice
¼ cup tequila
2 tablespoons seeded and finely
    chopped Vlasic hot jalapeno
    peppers

½ teaspoon grated orange peel
1 can (10½ ounces) Franco-
    American chicken gravy
3 whole chicken breasts, split

1. To make sauce: In 1-quart saucepan, combine juice, tequila, peppers and peel. Over high heat, heat to boiling. Reduce heat to low; simmer, uncovered, 10 minutes or until mixture is reduced by half. Add gravy; heat through, stirring constantly.

2. On grill rack, place chicken, skin side up, directly above medium coals. Grill, uncovered, 1 hour or until tender and juices run clear, turning and brushing often with sauce during the last 30 minutes. Makes 6 servings.

To broil: Arrange chicken, skin side up, on rack in broiler pan. Broil 6 inches from heat 40 minutes or until tender and juices run clear, turning and brushing often with sauce during the last 20 minutes.

Chicken 'n' Steak Fajitas

Ranch hands created the dish, fajitas, and named it after the meat they used—the then inexpensive and unwanted beef skirt steak (fajita in Spanish). Today, skirt steak is in such demand that many fajita recipes call for flank or round steak. To serve tortillas warm, heat them in foil on the grill. Pictured opposite.

½ cup dry white wine
½ cup Marie's classic herb
    vinaigrette
¼ cup soy sauce
1-pound beef flank steak
1 whole chicken breast, split,
    skinned and boned (½ pound
    boneless)
1 cup Marie's refrigerated avocado
    goddess salad dressing

1 Campbell's Fresh tomato,
    chopped
½ cup coarsely chopped onion
6 to 8 (8-inch) flour tortillas, heated
    Sliced pitted ripe olives
    Shredded Cheddar cheese
    Sour cream (optional)

1. To marinate: In large shallow nonmetal dish, combine wine, vinaigrette salad dressing and soy sauce. Add steak and chicken; turn to coat. Cover; refrigerate at least 4 hours or overnight, turning occasionally.

2. In medium bowl, combine avocado salad dressing, tomato and onion. Cover; refrigerate until serving time.

3. Drain steak and chicken. On grill rack, place steak and chicken directly above medium-hot coals. Grill, uncovered, until steak is desired doneness and chicken is tender (allow 10 minutes for rare steak, 14 minutes for medium steak and 15 minutes for chicken). Turn once during cooking.

4. To serve: Thinly slice steak and chicken into strips. Arrange strips down center of each tortilla. Top with avocado mixture, olives, cheese and sour cream, if desired. Wrap up. Makes 6 to 8 servings.

To broil: Arrange steak and chicken on rack in broiler pan. Broil 4 inches from heat until steak is desired doneness and chicken is tender (allow 12 minutes for rare steak, 14 minutes for medium steak and 15 minutes for chicken). Turn once during cooking.

Grilled Chicken Taco Salad

2 cups cubed grilled chicken
1 cup mild chunky salsa
4 cups shredded lettuce
1 can (28 ounces) Campbell's pork
    & beans in tomato sauce or
    2 cans (15½ ounces *each*)
    Campbell's Ranchero beans

1 cup crumbled tortilla chips
1 cup shredded Monterey Jack
    cheese (4 ounces)

In small bowl, combine chicken and salsa. In 2-quart glass bowl, layer half of the lettuce, beans, chicken mixture, tortilla chips and cheese. Repeat layers. Cover; refrigerate until serving time, at least 4 hours. Makes 10 cups or 8 servings.

Chicken 'n' Steak Fajitas

Tamale Pie

4 slices bacon
½ cup green pepper cut into 1-inch
    pieces
1 clove garlic, minced
1 tablespoon chili powder
2 cans (16 ounces *each*)
    Campbell's pork & beans in
    tomato sauce or 2 cans
    (15½ ounces *each*) Campbell's
    Ranchero beans

1 can (8 ounces) whole kernel
    golden corn, drained
1 egg
1 package (8½ to 12 ounces) corn
    muffin mix
⅓ cup milk

1. Preheat oven to 400°F. In 10-inch skillet over medium heat, cook bacon until crisp. Transfer to paper towels to drain. Crumble bacon. Spoon off all but 2 tablespoons drippings.

2. In hot drippings, cook pepper, garlic and chili powder until pepper is tender-crisp, stirring often. Stir in beans, corn and bacon; heat to boiling. Spoon bean mixture into 12- by 8-inch baking dish.

3. In small bowl, beat egg. Stir in muffin mix and milk. Spoon batter evenly over bean mixture. Bake, uncovered, 20 minutes or until top is golden brown. Makes 8 servings.

Bean-Stuffed Peppers

These peppers with a cheesy bean filling are a takeoff on Chiles Rellenos.

2 tablespoons vegetable oil
½ cup chopped onion
1 large clove garlic, minced
1 can (16 ounces) Campbell's pork
    & beans in tomato sauce
2 tablespoons chopped fresh
    cilantro

2 jars (16 ounces *each*) Vlasic
    sweet yellow bell peppers
1 cup shredded Monterey Jack
    cheese (4 ounces)

1. Preheat oven to 400°F. In 10-inch skillet over medium heat, in hot oil, cook onion and garlic until onion is tender, stirring often. Stir in beans and cilantro, pressing with spoon to mash beans. Cook, uncovered, 5 minutes or until thick, stirring occasionally.

2. Make a lengthwise slit in each pepper; remove seeds. Spoon bean mixture into peppers. Arrange stuffed peppers in 12- by 8-inch baking dish. Cover; bake 20 minutes. Uncover; sprinkle with cheese. Bake 1 minute more or until cheese is melted. Makes 10 to 12 servings.

Barbecue Beans

Double this recipe for the menu pictured on page 19.

1 tablespoon vegetable oil
1 medium onion, chopped
2 cans (16 ounces *each*)
    Campbell's pork & beans in
    tomato sauce
⅓ cup Open Pit original flavor
    barbecue sauce

1 tablespoon packed brown sugar
Vlasic cherry peppers for garnish
Vlasic banana pepper rings for
    garnish

In 10-inch skillet over medium heat, in hot oil, cook onion until tender, stirring often. Stir in beans, barbecue sauce and sugar. Over high heat, heat to boiling. Reduce heat to low; simmer, uncovered, 10 minutes, stirring occasionally. Garnish with peppers. Makes 4 cups or 8 servings.

To microwave: In 1½-quart microwave-safe casserole, combine oil and onion. Microwave, covered, on HIGH 3 minutes or until tender, stirring once. Stir in beans, barbecue sauce and sugar. Microwave, covered, on HIGH 8 minutes or until heated through, stirring twice.

Tex-Mex Bean Bake

Salsa, peppers and tortilla chips give this Texas bean dish a Mexican flair.

3 slices bacon, diced
½ cup chopped onion
½ cup green pepper cut into strips
1 clove garlic, minced
2 cans (16 ounces *each*)
    Campbell's pork & beans in
    tomato sauce or 2 cans
    (15½ ounces *each*) Campbell's
    Ranchero beans

¼ cup salsa
1 tablespoon seeded and chopped
    Vlasic hot jalapeno peppers
Crushed tortilla chips

1. In 10-inch skillet over medium heat, cook bacon, onion, green pepper and garlic until bacon is crisp and vegetables are tender, stirring often. Spoon off fat. Stir in beans, salsa and jalapeno peppers.

2. Transfer mixture to 1½-quart casserole. Bake, uncovered, at 350°F. 30 minutes or until heated through. Stir before serving. Sprinkle with tortilla chips. Makes 4 cups or 8 servings.

To microwave: In 1½-quart microwave-safe casserole, cover bacon with paper towel; microwave on HIGH 3 minutes. Stir in onion, green pepper and garlic. Microwave, covered with lid, on HIGH 3 minutes or until onion is tender, stirring once. Spoon off fat. Stir in beans, salsa and jalapeno peppers. Microwave, covered, on HIGH 8 minutes or until heated through, stirring twice.

Layered Tex-Mex Dip

Waiting for that meat to slow-cook? Share this make-ahead dip.

- **1 can (16 ounces) Campbell's pork & beans in tomato sauce**
- **⅓ cup salsa**
- **1 medium avocado, seeded and peeled**
- **2 teaspoons lemon juice**
- **1 large clove garlic, minced**
- **½ teaspoon ground cumin**
- **¼ teaspoon salt**
- **Sour cream for garnish**
- **Sliced pitted ripe olives for garnish**
- **Chopped Campbell's Fresh tomatoes for garnish**

1. In medium bowl, mash beans with fork. Stir in salsa. Spread in 8-inch glass pie plate. In medium bowl, mash avocado. Stir in lemon juice, garlic, cumin and salt. Mound in center over beans. Cover; refrigerate until serving time, at least 2 hours.

2. To serve: Garnish dip with sour cream, olives and tomatoes. Serve with tortilla chips for dipping. Makes 3 cups.

Cheesy Bean Dip

To keep the Tortilla Cup from softening, place a custard cup inside, then fill with dip.

- **1 or 2 Tortilla Cups (recipe follows)**
- **1 can (16 ounces) Campbell's pork & beans in tomato sauce**
- **¾ cup shredded Monterey Jack cheese (3 ounces)**
- **¼ cup seeded and chopped Vlasic pepperoncini salad peppers**
- **¼ cup chopped sweet red pepper**
- **1 tablespoon finely chopped onion**

1. Prepare Tortilla Cup. In small saucepan, coarsely mash beans with fork. Stir in cheese, peppers and onion. Over medium-high heat, heat until cheese is melted, stirring often.

2. To serve: Spoon dip into Tortilla Cup. Serve with crackers or chips for dipping. Makes 2½ cups.

To microwave: In 1-quart microwave-safe casserole, mash beans; stir in cheese, peppers and onion. Microwave, covered, on HIGH 3 minutes or until dip is hot and cheese is melted, stirring once.

TORTILLA CUP: Preheat oven to 400°F. On baking sheet, place 4-inch thick ball of foil. Spray 10-inch nonstick skillet with vegetable cooking spray. Over high heat, heat 1 (8-inch) flour tortilla 5 seconds on each side or until softened. Immediately drape tortilla over foil ball on baking sheet. Bake 5 minutes or until golden. Cool on foil. Makes 1 tortilla cup.

To microwave: Brush both sides of 1 (8-inch) flour tortilla with melted butter or margarine. Place over inverted 2-cup glass measure. Microwave on HIGH 30 seconds. Press tortilla to sides of measure. Microwave 30 seconds more. Cool on measure.

Cheesy Pepper Corn Bread

Double this easy recipe for the menu pictured on page 19.

1 package (8½ to 12 ounces) corn
   muffin mix
1 cup shredded Monterey Jack
   cheese (4 ounces)

2 to 3 teaspoons seeded and
   chopped Vlasic hot jalapeno or
   chili peppers

Prepare and bake corn muffin mix according to package directions, but stir cheese and peppers into batter. Cut into wedges or squares. Makes 8 servings.

Caramel Orange Flan

1¼ cups sugar, divided
8 eggs
4 cups milk

1 teaspoon vanilla extract
½ teaspoon grated orange peel

1. Preheat oven to 350°F. In 8-inch skillet over medium heat, melt ½ cup of the sugar until it forms a deep golden brown syrup, stirring constantly. Pour syrup onto bottom of 2-quart casserole.

2. In large bowl with mixer at medium speed, beat eggs and remaining ¾ cup sugar until thick and lemon colored. Gradually beat in milk, vanilla and peel. Slowly pour mixture over syrup in casserole.

3. Place large shallow baking pan on middle rack of oven. Carefully place casserole with mixture into baking pan. Fill baking pan with hot water to depth of 1 inch. Bake, uncovered, 1 hour and 20 minutes or until knife inserted in center comes out clean. Cool on wire rack. Cover; refrigerate until serving time, at least 4 hours.

4. To serve: With knife, loosen custard from sides of dish and invert onto serving plate, letting syrup run down sides onto dish. Cut into wedges. Makes 8 servings.

Mexican Wedding Cookies

These shortbread pecan cookies melt in your mouth. Pictured on page 19.

1½ cups confectioners' sugar,
   divided
1 cup butter or margarine,
   softened

¾ cup finely chopped pecans
½ teaspoon vanilla extract
2 cups all-purpose flour
¼ teaspoon ground cinnamon

1. Preheat oven to 350°F. Grease cookie sheets. In large bowl with mixer at medium speed, beat together 1 cup of the sugar, butter, pecans and vanilla. With spoon, stir in flour.

2. Shape dough into 1-inch balls, flatten slightly. Place on cookie sheets about 1 inch apart. Bake 12 to 15 minutes or until done but not browned. Cool 5 minutes on cookie sheets.

3. In small bowl, mix remaining ½ cup sugar and cinnamon. Gently toss each cookie in cinnamon mixture; cool on wire rack. Makes 40 cookies.

Burgers Pacific

Grilled Hawaiian pineapple tops these ginger-flavored burgers.

1½ pounds ground beef
⅓ cup chopped green onions
½ teaspoon ground ginger
⅛ teaspoon pepper
⅓ cup apricot preserves

⅓ cup Open Pit original flavor
   barbecue sauce
6 pineapple slices
6 hamburger buns, split and
   toasted

1. In large bowl, combine beef, onions, ginger and pepper. Shape into six 1-inch-thick patties.

2. To make sauce: In small saucepan, combine preserves and barbecue sauce. Over medium heat, heat to boiling, stirring often.

3. On grill rack, place patties directly above medium coals. Grill, uncovered, until desired doneness (allow 10 minutes for medium and 12 minutes for well-done), turning and brushing often with sauce. Place pineapple on grill; grill 1 minute or until browned, turning once.

4. To serve: Place patties on buns with pineapple. Makes 6 servings.

To broil: Arrange patties on rack in broiler pan. Broil 4 inches from heat until desired doneness (allow 15 minutes for medium and 18 minutes for well-done), turning and brushing often with sauce. Broil pineapple 1 minute, turning once.

Rosemary Lamb Riblets

1 tablespoon vegetable oil
¼ cup finely chopped onion
2 cloves garlic, minced
1 teaspoon dried rosemary leaves,
   crushed

1 cup Open Pit original flavor
   barbecue sauce
2 pounds lamb breast riblets
   (about 12), cut into serving
   pieces

1. To make sauce: In 1-quart saucepan over medium heat, in hot oil, cook onion, garlic and rosemary until onion is tender, stirring often. Stir in barbecue sauce; heat through, stirring occasionally.

2. In covered grill, arrange preheated coals around drip pan; test for medium heat above pan.

3. On grill rack, place ribs, fat side up, over pan but not over coals. Grill, covered, 1¼ hours or until tender. Adjust vents and add more charcoal as necessary. Turn and brush often with sauce during the last 45 minutes. Makes 2 to 3 servings.

> *A clean grill is a safe grill, from a food or fire safety standpoint. Follow your grill manufacturer's directions for cleaning and clean it often. To speed clean-up, line the fire box with heavy-duty foil and coat cold grids with vegetable cooking spray or vegetable oil before cooking.*

Grilled Chicken with Melon Sauce

Sun-ripened melon and kiwifruit star in this California-style entree.

1 teaspoon grated orange peel	2 kiwifruit, peeled and chopped
⅓ cup orange juice	1 cup finely chopped cantaloupe
1 tablespoon vegetable oil	⅓ cup Open Pit original flavor
3 whole chicken breasts, split,	barbecue sauce
skinned and boned	1 tablespoon packed brown sugar
(1½ pounds boneless)	2 teaspoons cornstarch

1. To marinate: In large shallow nonmetal dish, combine peel, juice and oil. Add chicken; turn to coat. Cover; refrigerate at least 4 hours or overnight, turning occasionally.

2. Drain chicken, reserving marinade. On grill rack, place chicken directly above medium-hot coals. Grill, uncovered, 12 to 14 minutes or until tender and juices run clear, turning once.

3. To make sauce: In 1-quart saucepan, combine reserved marinade, kiwifruit, cantaloupe, barbecue sauce, sugar and cornstarch; stir until smooth. Over medium heat, heat until mixture boils and thickens, stirring constantly. Serve over chicken. Makes 6 servings.

To broil: Arrange chicken on rack in broiler pan. Broil 4 inches from heat 15 minutes or until tender and juices run clear, turning once.

Chinatown Chicken Wings

Ginger and soy sauce add a flavor reminiscent of San Francisco's Chinatown.

¾ cup Open Pit original flavor	½ teaspoon ground ginger
barbecue sauce	18 chicken wings (about 3 pounds)
3 tablespoons soy sauce	Vegetable oil
1 large clove garlic, minced	

1. To make sauce: In medium bowl, combine barbecue sauce, soy sauce, garlic and ginger.

2. Cut tips off chicken wings; discard tips or save for another use. Cut wings at joints to form 36 pieces; brush with oil.

3. Brush grill rack with oil. On grill rack, place wings directly above medium coals. Grill, uncovered, 30 minutes or until tender and juices run clear, turning and brushing often with sauce during the last 15 minutes. Makes 36 appetizers.

To broil: Arrange wings on rack in broiler pan. Broil 6 inches from heat 40 minutes or until tender and juices run clear, turning and brushing often with sauce during the last 15 minutes.

Citrus-Mushroom-Spinach Salad

A splash of basil vinaigrette accents this summery salad. Pictured on page 37.

1 package (8 ounces) Campbell's
    Fresh mushrooms, sliced
    (3 cups)
2 oranges, peeled and sectioned
½ cup pitted ripe olives, halved
2 tablespoons thinly sliced green
    onion
2 tablespoons olive oil

1 tablespoon wine vinegar
1 tablespoon chopped fresh basil
    leaves or ½ teaspoon dried
    basil leaves, crushed
½ teaspoon salt
    Dash pepper
2 cups packed torn spinach leaves

1. In medium bowl, combine mushrooms, oranges, olives, onion, oil, vinegar, basil, salt and pepper; toss gently to coat. Cover; refrigerate until serving time, at least 2 hours.

2. To serve: In large serving bowl, combine mushroom mixture and spinach; toss gently to coat. Makes 5 cups or 5 servings.

Tarragon Marinated Mushrooms

If you don't have the tarragon vinegar called for in this recipe, use white vinegar and one teaspoon of dried tarragon, crushed.

6 tablespoons olive oil, divided
1 package (3.5 ounces)
    Campbell's Fresh oyster
    mushrooms, each cut in half or
    1 package (8 ounces)
    Campbell's Fresh mushrooms,
    sliced
1 cup thinly sliced carrots
1 small sweet red pepper, cut into
    1-inch squares (about ⅔ cup)

2 tablespoons tarragon vinegar
2 teaspoons Dijon-style mustard
1 clove garlic, minced
½ to 1 teaspoon dried tarragon
    leaves, crushed
    Salad greens
    Chopped fresh parsley for
    garnish

1. In 2-quart saucepan over high heat, in 2 tablespoons hot oil, cook mushrooms until lightly browned, stirring often. Remove from pan. In same saucepan over high heat, cook carrots and pepper until tender-crisp, stirring occasionally. Remove from pan.

2. In same saucepan over medium heat, with fork or wire whisk, beat together remaining 4 tablespoons oil, vinegar and mustard until smooth. Stir in cooked vegetables, garlic and tarragon. Simmer, covered, 5 minutes. Refrigerate, covered, until serving time, at least 4 hours.

3. To serve: With slotted spoon, serve mushroom mixture on salad greens. Garnish with parsley. Makes 2 cups or 3 servings.

To microwave: Decrease oil to 5 tablespoons. In 2-quart microwave-safe casserole, combine carrots, pepper, and 1 tablespoon oil. Microwave, covered, on HIGH 4 minutes or until tender-crisp, stirring once. Add mushrooms; microwave, covered, on HIGH 1 minute. Whisk together remaining 4 tablespoons oil, vinegar, mustard, garlic and tarragon; stir into vegetables. Microwave, covered, on HIGH 3 minutes, stirring once.

Creamy Dill Bean Dip

Flecks of carrot and zucchini color this sour cream and dill dip.

1 can (16 ounces) Campbell's pork
  & beans in tomato sauce
1 cup shredded zucchini
½ cup shredded carrot

¼ cup Marie's refrigerated sour
  cream and dill salad dressing
1 teaspoon lemon juice
Carrot curls for garnish

1. In medium bowl, coarsely mash beans with fork. Stir in zucchini, carrot, salad dressing and juice. Cover; refrigerate until serving time, at least 2 hours.

2. To serve: Garnish dip with carrot curls. Serve with tortilla chips or crackers for dipping. Makes 2½ cups.

Sunset Yogurt Dip

Serve with fresh strawberries or other fruit as pictured on page 37.

1 cup plain yogurt
¼ cup confectioners' sugar
½ teaspoon grated orange peel

¼ teaspoon vanilla extract
Orange peel for garnish
Fresh strawberry for garnish

In small bowl, combine yogurt, sugar, grated peel and vanilla; stir until smooth. Cover; refrigerate until serving time. Garnish with orange peel and fresh strawberry. Serve with fresh strawberries or chilled fruit for dipping. Makes 1 cup.

Fresh Fruit Ambrosia

This easy fruit toss also tastes great with grilled chicken or pork.

2 tablespoons lime juice
1 tablespoon honey
2 oranges, peeled and sliced
2 kiwifruit, peeled and sliced

2 bananas, peeled and sliced
1 cup seedless red grapes
Toasted coconut

In medium bowl, combine lime juice and honey. Add oranges, kiwifruit, bananas and grapes; toss gently to coat. Cover; refrigerate until serving time, at least 30 minutes, but no longer than 4 hours. Sprinkle with coconut. Makes 6 cups or 8 servings.

Honey-Glazed Country-Style Ribs

For a change, try this recipe with Open Pit hickory barbecue sauce.

1 tablespoon vegetable oil
½ cup finely chopped onion
2 cloves garlic, minced
1 cup Open Pit original flavor barbecue sauce

⅓ cup honey
5 pounds pork country-style ribs

1. To make sauce: In 2-quart saucepan over medium heat, in hot oil, cook onion and garlic until onion is tender, stirring often. Stir in barbecue sauce and honey. Heat to boiling. Reduce heat to low; simmer, uncovered, 10 minutes, stirring occasionally.

2. In covered grill, arrange preheated coals around drip pan; test for medium heat above pan.

3. On grill rack, place ribs, fat side up, over pan but not over coals. Grill, covered, 1½ to 2 hours or until well-done. Adjust vents and add more charcoal as necessary. Turn and brush with sauce every 30 minutes. Makes 10 servings.

To roast: Place ribs, fat side up, on rack in roasting pan. Roast, uncovered, at 350°F. 1½ to 2 hours or until well-done. Turn and brush often with sauce during the last 30 minutes.

Apple-Glazed Pork Chops

This grilled chop showcases apple products from the northern states. Pictured on page 49 and on back cover.

1 can (10¼ ounces) Franco-American beef gravy
¼ cup apple jelly
1 tablespoon cider vinegar
¼ teaspoon ground cloves
⅛ teaspoon pepper

6 pork chops, each cut ¾ inch thick
Grapes for garnish
Apple slices for garnish
Fresh oregano for garnish

1. To make glaze: In 1½-quart saucepan, combine gravy, jelly, vinegar, cloves and pepper. Over medium-high heat, heat to boiling, stirring constantly.

2. On grill rack, place chops directly above medium coals. Grill, uncovered, 20 minutes or until well-done, turning and brushing often with glaze during the last 15 minutes.

3. To serve: Heat any remaining glaze; serve with chops. Garnish with grapes, apple slices and oregano. Makes 6 servings.

To broil: Arrange chops on rack in broiler pan. Broil 4 inches from heat 20 to 30 minutes or until well-done, turning and brushing often with glaze during the last 10 minutes.

Mushroom-Stuffed Iowa Chops

The champion pork-producing state of Iowa often lends its name to the thick pork rib chop used for stuffing.

1 tablespoon butter or margarine
2 cups thinly sliced Campbell's Fresh mushrooms
½ cup shredded carrot
⅓ cup sliced green onions
2 tablespoons chopped fresh parsley
1 tablespoon lemon juice
¼ teaspoon rubbed sage

Dash pepper
4 pork rib chops, each cut 1½ inches thick
1 tablespoon vegetable oil
½ teaspoon dried thyme leaves, crushed
½ cup Open Pit original flavor barbecue sauce

1. To make filling: In 10-inch skillet over medium heat, in hot butter, cook mushrooms until tender, stirring occasionally. Remove from heat. Stir in carrot, onions, parsley, juice, sage and pepper.

2. Make a pocket in each chop by cutting horizontally from fat side to bone. Fill each chop with ¼ cup of the filling, pressing firmly into opening. Secure with toothpicks. Brush chops with oil. Rub thyme over chops.

3. On grill rack, place chops directly above medium coals. Grill, uncovered, 35 to 40 minutes or until well-done, turning and brushing often with barbecue sauce during the last 20 minutes. Makes 4 servings.

To broil: Arrange chops on rack in broiler pan. Broil 4 inches from heat 25 to 30 minutes or until well-done, turning and brushing often with barbecue sauce during the last 10 minutes.

Down-Home Chicken Grill

You'll find corn served many ways in the Heartland, on the cob and off. Here it meets chicken and beans for a four-ingredient main dish.

6 chicken legs (about 2 pounds)
¾ cup Open Pit original flavor barbecue sauce, divided
2 cans (16 ounces *each*) Campbell's pork & beans in tomato sauce

1 can (8 ounces) whole kernel golden corn, drained

1. On grill rack, place chicken, skin side down, directly above medium coals. Grill, uncovered, 1 hour or until tender and juices run clear. Turn and brush often with ½ cup of the barbecue sauce during the last 30 minutes.

2. Meanwhile, in 10-inch cast-iron skillet combine beans, corn and remaining ¼ cup barbecue sauce. Place on grill for the last 15 minutes or until hot, stirring occasionally. Add chicken to skillet; spoon mixture over. Makes 6 servings.

To roast: Decrease barbecue sauce to ¼ cup. Arrange chicken, skin side down, in 12- by 8-inch baking dish. Bake, uncovered, at 400°F. 40 minutes, turning after 20 minutes. Spoon off fat. In bowl, combine beans, corn and 2 tablespoons barbecue sauce; spoon around chicken. Brush chicken with 2 tablespoons barbecue sauce. Bake 20 minutes more or until chicken is tender and juices run clear.

Country Slaw

Pickles offer an easy shortcut to vinaigrette-style slaw. Pictured on page 49.

1 cup Vlasic sweet salad cubes
4 cups shredded cabbage

½ cup sliced celery
⅓ cup shredded carrot

In medium bowl, combine all ingredients. Cover; refrigerate until serving time, at least 2 hours, stirring occasionally. Makes 4 cups or 6 servings.

Ham-Stuffed Mushrooms

½ package (4 ounces) cream
   cheese, softened
¼ cup Marie's refrigerated sour
   cream and dill salad dressing
¼ cup finely chopped cooked ham
3 tablespoons finely chopped
   celery
2 tablespoons finely chopped
   green onion

2 tablespoons *drained* Vlasic
   sweet relish
1 package (16 ounces) Campbell's
   Fresh gourmet stuffing
   mushrooms
Chopped fresh parsley for
   garnish

In medium bowl, stir cream cheese until smooth; stir in salad dressing until blended. Stir in ham, celery, onion and relish. Cover; refrigerate until serving time, at least 2 hours. Remove mushroom stems and reserve for another use. Spoon about 2 teaspoons filling into each mushroom cap. Garnish with chopped parsley. Makes 1 cup filling or 20 appetizers.

Lattice-Topped Strawberry-Rhubarb Pie

Nicknamed "pieplant" because it's often baked in pies, fresh rhubarb, as used in this recipe, is most widely available from February through July. Pictured on page 49.

2 cups rhubarb cut into ½-inch
   pieces
2 cups sliced strawberries
1 cup sugar
⅓ cup all-purpose flour

Pastry for 2-crust 9-inch pie
2 tablespoons butter or margarine
1 egg yolk
1 tablespoon water

1. Preheat oven to 375°F. In large bowl, combine rhubarb, strawberries, sugar and flour; toss to coat.

2. Roll out half of the pastry to fit 9-inch pie plate. Spread fruit filling over pie crust. Dot with butter. Roll out remaining pastry to 10-inch circle. Cut into 1-inch-wide strips. Arrange strips over filling in lattice pattern. Trim, seal and flute edges. Combine egg yolk and water; brush onto pastry.

3. Bake, uncovered, 30 minutes. Cover edge of pie with foil; bake 15 minutes more or until crust is golden. Cool on wire rack. Makes 8 servings.

Creamy Blue Cheese Dip

½ cup Marie's refrigerated regular
or lite blue cheese salad
dressing
½ cup Marie's refrigerated sour
cream and dill salad dressing

2 tablespoons thinly sliced green
onion
1 teaspoon lemon juice

In small bowl, combine all ingredients. Serve with vegetables or crackers for dipping. Makes 1 cup.

Grilled Raisin-Stuffed Apples

Use firm apples, such as Rome Beauty, Granny Smith, Winesap or Golden Delicious.

½ cup raisins
¼ cup chopped walnuts
2 tablespoons packed brown
sugar

2 teaspoons ground cinnamon
6 medium cooking apples, cored
6 caramels

1. In small bowl, combine raisins, walnuts, sugar and cinnamon. Divide among apple centers. Press one caramel into each apple. Place 1 apple on 15- by 12-inch piece of heavy-duty foil. Bring edges of foil together; seal loosely. Repeat, making 6 bundles.

2. On grill rack, place bundles, seam side up, directly above medium coals. Grill 45 minutes or until fork-tender. Makes 6 servings.

Old-Fashioned Strawberry Shortcake

1¾ cups all-purpose flour
⅓ cup sugar, divided
1 tablespoon baking powder
½ teaspoon salt
¼ teaspoon ground nutmeg
5 tablespoons butter or margarine,
divided

1 egg
½ cup milk
2 cups sliced strawberries
1 cup sweetened whipped cream
Fresh strawberries for garnish

1. Preheat oven to 450°F. Grease 8-inch round cake pan. In bowl, stir together flour, 2 tablespoons of the sugar, baking powder, salt and nutmeg. With pastry blender or fork, cut in 4 tablespoons butter until mixture resembles coarse crumbs.

2. In small bowl, with fork, beat egg; stir in milk. Add egg mixture to flour mixture. With fork, mix just until mixture forms a soft dough that leaves sides of bowl.

3. Turn dough onto lightly floured surface; knead 10 strokes until mixed. Divide dough into two portions; pat one portion in pan. Place remaining 1 tablespoon butter in center; pat remaining dough over top almost to edge. Bake 20 minutes or until golden brown. Remove from pan; cool on wire rack 10 minutes.

4. To serve: In medium bowl, combine sliced strawberries and remaining sugar. Split shortcake into two layers. Spoon half of the berries onto bottom layer; top with top layer. Spoon remaining berries on top. Top with whipped cream. Garnish with additional berries. Makes 8 servings.

Crab-Stuffed Trout

Fresh crab is a staple for many Chesapeake Bay area cooks. Pictured on page 63.

⅓ cup butter or margarine, divided
2 cups chopped Campbell's Fresh
  mushrooms
½ cup finely chopped onion
½ cup shredded carrot
1 cup crabmeat, flaked
¼ cup fine dry bread crumbs
3 tablespoons chopped fresh
  parsley, divided

1 tablespoon white wine
  Worcestershire sauce
6 brook trout or salmon (8 ounces
  each), pan-dressed
2 teaspoons lemon juice
  Arugula for garnish
  Cherry tomatoes for garnish

1. To make filling: In 10-inch skillet over medium heat, in 3 tablespoons hot butter, cook mushrooms, onion and carrot until tender and liquid has evaporated, stirring occasionally. In medium bowl, combine onion mixture, crabmeat, crumbs, 2 tablespoons of the parsley and Worcestershire; toss gently to coat. Spoon ½ cup filling loosely into each fish cavity; secure with toothpicks.

2. Arrange fish in oiled grill basket. In covered grill, arrange preheated coals around drip pan; test for hot coals above pan. On grill rack, place grill basket over pan but not over coals. Cover; grill 16 to 20 minutes or until fish begins to flake when tested with fork, turning once.

3. In 1-quart saucepan, combine remaining butter, remaining parsley and juice. Heat until butter is melted, stirring occasionally. Garnish with arugula and tomatoes. Serve with sauce. Makes 6 servings.

To broil: Arrange fish on rack in broiler pan. Broil 6 inches from heat 16 to 20 minutes or until fish begins to flake when tested with fork, turning once.

Zesty Cocktail Sauce

Grill seafood on skewers to serve with this barbecue-sauce-based dip.

¾ cup Open Pit original flavor
  barbecue sauce
2 tablespoons prepared
  horseradish

1 tablespoon sugar
1 tablespoon lemon juice

In small bowl, combine all ingredients. Cover; refrigerate until serving time, at least 2 hours. Serve with grilled or boiled shellfish for dipping. Makes 1 cup.

Creamy Tartar Sauce

½ cup Marie's refrigerated regular
  ranch salad dressing

2 tablespoons Vlasic India or
  sweet relish
½ teaspoon lemon juice

In small bowl, combine all ingredients. Cover; refrigerate until serving time. Serve with grilled or fried seafood for dipping. Makes about ½ cup.

Corn-Stuffed Chicken

Be sure to pack the stuffing loosely in the bird so it will heat through. You can foil-wrap and heat any remaining stuffing on the grill.

¼ cup butter or margarine
½ cup chopped onion
½ cup sliced celery
½ teaspoon dried thyme leaves, crushed
4 cups fresh bread cubes

1 cup whole kernel corn, cooked
2 cans (10½ ounces *each*) Franco-American chicken gravy, divided
¼ teaspoon pepper
5-pound roasting chicken

1. To make stuffing: In 1½-quart saucepan over medium heat, in hot butter, cook onion, celery and thyme until tender, stirring often. In large bowl, combine onion mixture, bread, corn, ¼ cup of the gravy and pepper; toss gently to coat.

2. Remove neck and giblets from inside bird. Remove excess fat. Cut off and discard neck skin. Rinse bird with cold running water; drain well. Spoon stuffing loosely into body cavity. Fold skin over stuffing; secure with skewer. With breast side up, lift wings toward neck, then fold tips under back of bird. Tie legs.

3. In covered grill, arrange preheated coals around drip pan; test for medium heat above pan. Insert meat thermometer into thickest part of meat between breast and thigh, without touching fat or bone.

4. On grill rack, place chicken, breast side up, over pan but not over coals. Grill, covered, 2 to 2½ hours or until well-done or 180°F. Adjust vents and add more charcoal as necessary.

5. To make sauce: Remove chicken from grill, reserving 2 tablespoons drippings. In 1-quart saucepan, combine remaining gravy and reserved drippings. Over medium heat, heat through, stirring constantly. Serve sauce with chicken. Makes 8 to 10 servings.

To roast: Place stuffed bird, breast side up, on rack in roasting pan. Roast, uncovered, at 325°F. 2½ to 3 hours or until well-done or 180°F.

Succotash

Pork & beans add a new twist to this colonial corn-and-lima favorite.

1 tablespoon butter or margarine
½ cup chopped onion
¼ teaspoon dried thyme leaves, crushed
1 can (16 ounces) Campbell's pork & beans in tomato sauce

1 cup succotash (½ cup *each* whole kernel corn and baby lima beans), cooked
2 tablespoons chopped fresh parsley

In 3-quart saucepan over medium heat, in hot butter, cook onion and thyme until tender, stirring often. Stir in beans, succotash and parsley. Heat through, stirring occasionally. Makes 3 cups or 6 servings.

To microwave: In 1½-quart microwave-safe casserole, combine butter, onion and thyme. Microwave, covered, on HIGH 3 minutes or until tender, stirring once. Stir in beans, succotash and parsley. Microwave, covered, on HIGH 5 minutes or until heated through, stirring twice.

Dilled Crab Salad Mold

1 envelope unflavored gelatin
1 cup water
½ cup Marie's refrigerated sour
    cream and dill salad dressing
1 tablespoon finely chopped onion
    Dash hot pepper sauce

2 cups crabmeat, flaked
½ cup chopped Vlasic mild banana
    pepper rings
1 cup heavy cream, whipped
    Campbell's Fresh butterhead
    lettuce leaves

1. In medium saucepan, sprinkle gelatin over water to soften; let stand 1 minute. Over low heat, heat until gelatin is dissolved, stirring constantly. Do not boil.

2. In medium bowl, combine salad dressing, onion and hot pepper sauce. Gradually stir in gelatin mixture. Cover; refrigerate about 40 minutes or until mixture mounds slightly when dropped from spoon.

3. Gently fold crabmeat and peppers into gelatin mixture. Fold in whipped cream. Pour into 4-cup mold. Cover; refrigerate until set, at least 2 hours.

4. To serve: Unmold onto lettuce-lined serving platter. Serve with crackers. Makes 4 cups.

Blueberry-Walnut-Orange Muffins

If you miss blueberry season, June through September, use unthawed frozen blueberries for this recipe.

1¾ cups all-purpose flour
⅓ cup sugar
2 teaspoons baking powder
½ teaspoon baking soda
½ teaspoon salt
1 egg

1 teaspoon grated orange peel
1 cup orange juice
¼ cup vegetable oil
1 cup fresh or frozen blueberries
½ cup chopped walnuts

1. Preheat oven to 400°F. Line 12 (2½-inch) baking cups with paper baking cups. In large bowl, stir together flour, sugar, baking powder, baking soda and salt.

2. In small bowl, beat egg. Add peel, juice and oil; stir until blended. Add orange mixture to flour mixture, stirring just until moistened. Fold in blueberries and walnuts.

3. Fill prepared muffin cups ⅔ full with batter. Bake 20 minutes or until toothpick inserted in centers comes out clean. Let muffins stand 2 minutes; remove from muffin pan. Cool slightly on wire racks. Serve warm. Makes 12 muffins.

Sour Cream Cheesecake

A sour cream glaze tops this New York specialty. Pictured on page 63.

2 cups graham cracker or zwieback crumbs
⅓ cup butter or margarine, melted
3 packages (8 ounces *each*) cream cheese, softened
1¼ cups sugar, divided
4 eggs
1 teaspoon grated lemon peel
1½ teaspoons vanilla extract, divided
Generous dash salt
1 cup sour cream
Fresh raspberries for garnish
Fresh mint for garnish

1. To make crust: In small bowl, combine crumbs and butter. Press mixture firmly onto bottom and 1½ inches up side of 9-inch springform pan.

2. In large bowl with mixer at medium speed, beat cream cheese until light and fluffy. Add 1 cup of the sugar; beat until mixed. Add eggs, peel, 1 teaspoon of the vanilla and salt; beat until very smooth. Pour mixture into crumb crust. Bake at 325°F. 1 hour or until center is just set. Cool on wire rack 20 minutes.

3. To make topping: In small bowl, combine sour cream, remaining ¼ cup sugar and ½ teaspoon vanilla. Spread over cheesecake. Bake 10 minutes more. Cool on wire rack. Cover; refrigerate until serving time, at least 8 hours. Garnish with raspberries and mint. Makes 12 servings.

Lemon-Blueberry Tart

2 pints fresh blueberries, divided
¾ cup sugar
4 teaspoons cornstarch
1 tablespoon lemon juice
2 packages (3 ounces *each*) cream cheese, softened
2 tablespoons milk
1 teaspoon grated lemon peel
9-inch baked pie crust

1. In covered blender or food processor, puree 1 pint of the blueberries, 1 cup at a time, until almost smooth.

2. In 2-quart saucepan, stir together sugar and cornstarch. Stir in pureed berries, remaining 1 pint berries and juice. Over medium heat, cook until mixture boils and thickens, stirring constantly. Cook 2 minutes more, stirring constantly. Remove from heat; cool to room temperature.

3. In small bowl with mixer at medium speed, combine cream cheese, milk and peel; beat until smooth. Spread over bottom of crust. Spoon cooled blueberry mixture over cheese layer. Cover; refrigerate until serving time, at least 12 hours. Makes 8 servings.

Burgers U.S.A.

What could be more American than the humble meat patty in a bun? It's best grilled and served with relish, pickles, lettuce, tomatoes and onion.

1½ pounds ground beef
⅓ cup Open Pit original flavor barbecue sauce, divided
2 tablespoons finely chopped onion
½ teaspoon dried basil leaves, crushed

½ teaspoon dried oregano leaves, crushed
6 hamburger buns, split and toasted
Vlasic original hamburger dill chips or hamburger relish

1. In large bowl, combine beef, 2 tablespoons of the barbecue sauce, onion, basil and oregano. Shape into six 1-inch-thick patties.

2. On grill rack, place patties directly above medium coals. Grill, uncovered, until desired doneness (allow 10 minutes for medium and 12 minutes for well-done), turning and brushing often with remaining barbecue sauce.

3. To serve: Place patties on buns with dill chips. Makes 6 servings.

To broil: Arrange patties on rack in broiler pan. Broil 4 inches from heat until desired doneness (allow 15 minutes for medium and 18 minutes for well-done), turning and brushing often with remaining barbecue sauce.

Inside-Out Burgers

You'll find cheese and pickles tucked inside these grilled burgers.

1 pound ground beef
½ cup shredded sharp Cheddar cheese (2 ounces)
12 Vlasic bread & butter pickles

¼ cup Open Pit original flavor barbecue sauce
4 hamburger buns, split and toasted

1. Divide beef into 8 portions; shape each portion into a ½-inch-thick patty. Place 2 tablespoons cheese and 3 pickle slices in centers of 4 patties. Top with remaining 4 patties; pinch to seal.

2. On grill rack, place filled patties directly above medium coals. Grill, uncovered, until desired doneness (allow 10 minutes for medium and 12 minutes for well-done), turning and brushing often with barbecue sauce.

3. To serve: Place patties on buns. Makes 4 servings.

To broil: Arrange patties on rack in broiler pan. Broil 4 inches from heat until desired doneness (allow 15 minutes for medium and 18 minutes for well-done), turning and brushing often with barbecue sauce.

Barbecued Chicken

Chicken bathed in a spunky barbecue sauce is a surefire crowd-pleaser. In fact, it may be no coincidence that the national preference for chicken is growing right along with grill sales. Pictured on page 75.

2 cloves garlic, minced
¼ teaspoon salt
**2 broiler-fryer chickens, (2½ to
  3 pounds *each*), quartered**

**½ cup Open Pit original flavor
  barbecue sauce**
Celery leaves for garnish

1. In small bowl, combine garlic and salt. With finger, loosen skin from chicken; rub garlic mixture on meat under skin of each piece.

2. On grill rack, place chicken, skin side down, directly above medium coals. Grill, uncovered, 1 hour or until tender and juices run clear, turning and brushing with barbecue sauce every 10 minutes. Garnish with celery leaves. Makes 8 servings.

To broil: Arrange chicken, skin side down, on rack in broiler pan. Broil 6 inches from heat 40 minutes or until tender and juices run clear, turning and brushing with barbecue sauce after 30 minutes.

Currant-Glazed Cornish Hens

The tender Cornish game hen, Yankee ingenuity at its best, is a cross between an American hen and a British rooster. The gravy-based glaze also tastes great on chicken.

**1 can (10½ ounces) Franco-
  American chicken gravy**
½ cup red currant jelly

1 tablespoon Dijon-style mustard
1 teaspoon grated orange peel
3 Cornish hens (1½ pounds *each*)

1. To make glaze: In 1-quart saucepan, combine gravy, jelly, mustard and peel. Over medium heat, heat to boiling, stirring often. Reduce heat to low; simmer, uncovered, 5 minutes, stirring constantly.

2. Remove neck and giblets from inside hens. Cut in half lengthwise. Rinse halves with cold running water; pat dry. Sprinkle with salt and pepper.

3. On grill rack, place hens, skin side up, directly above medium coals. Grill, uncovered, 30 to 40 minutes or until tender and juices run clear, turning and brushing often with glaze. Makes 6 servings.

To broil: Arrange hens, skin side down, on rack in broiler pan. Broil 6 inches from heat 30 minutes or until tender and juices run clear, turning and brushing often with glaze.

When grilling food directly over coals, watch for flare-ups. A breeze hitting fat-splashed coals may fan flames and char your dinner. To prevent fires, trim as much fat from meat as possible and clean the grill often. If fires occur, remove the food and spritz the grill with a spray bottle of water.

Hickory-Smoked Turkey Breast

The turkey is not our national bird as Ben Franklin would have wished, but it is perfect for picking up the flavor from smoldering hickory chips. Try grilling with orange, cherry or grapevine woods too.

Hickory chips
½ teaspoon salt
½ teaspoon rubbed sage

7 pounds frozen whole turkey breast, thawed
½ cup Open Pit original flavor barbecue sauce

1. At least 1 hour before grilling, soak wood chips in enough water to cover. Drain wood chips.

2. In small bowl, combine salt and sage. With finger, loosen skin from turkey; rub sage mixture on meat under skin.

3. In covered grill, arrange preheated coals around drip pan; test for medium heat above pan. Sprinkle 4 cups of the wood chips over coals. Insert a meat thermometer into thickest part of breast, without touching fat or bone.

4. On grill rack, place turkey, skin side up, over pan but not over coals. Grill, covered, 1½ to 2 hours or until well-done or 170°F. Adjust vents and add more charcoal and wood chips as necessary. Brush often with barbecue sauce during the last 30 minutes. Let stand 10 minutes before serving. Makes 14 servings.

Easy Franks 'n' Beans

Kids of all ages love this quick range-top bean dish.

2 cans (16 ounces *each*) Campbell's pork & beans in tomato sauce
4 frankfurters, thickly sliced
3 green onions, sliced

1 tablespoon prepared mustard
¼ teaspoon pepper
½ cup shredded sharp Cheddar cheese (2 ounces)

In 10-inch skillet, combine beans, frankfurters, onions, mustard and pepper. Over medium heat, heat to boiling. Reduce heat to low; simmer, uncovered, 10 minutes, stirring occasionally. Top with cheese; heat until cheese is melted. Makes 4 cups or 4 servings.

To microwave: In 1½-quart microwave-safe casserole, combine beans, frankfurters, onions, mustard and pepper. Microwave, covered, on HIGH 7 minutes or until heated through, stirring twice. Top with cheese; microwave, uncovered, on HIGH 1 minute or until cheese is melted.

Classic Baked Beans

Baked beans were served first as an Indian dish, then as a colonial staple, now as standard barbecue fare. Pictured on page 75.

2 cans (16 ounces *each*)
    Campbell's pork & beans in
    tomato sauce
½ cup finely chopped onion
⅓ cup ketchup

2 tablespoons packed brown
    sugar
1 tablespoon prepared mustard
4 slices bacon, cut in half and
    partially cooked

In 1½-quart casserole, combine beans, onion, ketchup, sugar and mustard. Top with bacon. Bake, uncovered, at 350°F. 1 hour or until hot and bubbly. Stir before serving. Makes 3½ cups or 6 to 8 servings.

To microwave: Starting with uncooked bacon, in 1½-quart microwave-safe casserole, cover bacon with paper towel; microwave on HIGH 4 minutes or until crisp, stirring once. Transfer bacon to paper towels to drain. Spoon off all but 1 teaspoon drippings. Add onion to drippings; microwave, covered with lid, on HIGH 3 minutes, stirring once. Stir in beans, ketchup, sugar, mustard and bacon. Microwave, covered, on HIGH 8 minutes or until heated through, stirring twice.

Parmesan Bread Deluxe

Reheat any leftover bread on the grill or in a microwave oven. Pictured on page 75.

¾ cup grated Parmesan cheese
⅓ cup Marie's refrigerated regular
    ranch, blue cheese, sour
    cream and dill, Italian garlic or
    buttermilk spice ranch style
    salad dressing

3 tablespoons finely chopped
    onion
1 loaf (8 ounces) Italian bread, cut
    into ½-inch-thick slices

In small bowl, combine cheese, salad dressing and onion. Spread a generous teaspoon of the dressing mixture onto one side of each bread slice. Arrange bread, spread side up, on cookie sheets. Broil 4 inches from heat 2 minutes or until golden brown. Makes about 24 slices.

> *Grill vegetables alongside your meat for an easy meal. Use heavy-duty foil to wrap corn-on-the-cob, whole potatoes or a mixture of cut-up fresh or frozen vegetables. Seal tightly and grill directly over medium coals until tender, about 40 to 60 minutes for corn and potatoes and 20 to 30 minutes for other vegetables. Remove the foil carefully as steam will escape.*

Fudge Brownies

A pan of sinfully rich brownies makes a perfect picnic tote-along.

¾ cup all-purpose flour
½ teaspoon baking powder
½ cup butter or margarine
1 cup sugar
2 eggs

2 squares (1 ounce *each*)
   unsweetened chocolate,
   melted and cooled
1 teaspoon vanilla extract
½ cup chopped pecans or walnuts

1. Grease 8- by 8-inch baking pan. In small bowl, stir together flour and baking powder.

2. In medium bowl with mixer at medium speed, beat together butter and sugar until light and fluffy. Add eggs, chocolate and vanilla; beat until mixed, scraping bowl often. Add flour mixture to chocolate mixture; stir until combined. Gently fold in nuts.

3. Spread batter in pan. Bake at 350°F. 30 minutes or until top springs back when touched lightly with finger. Cool on wire rack. Cut into squares. Makes 12 servings.

Peanut Butter Brownies: Substitute ½ cup peanut butter-flavored pieces for walnuts.

Mint Brownies: Substitute ½ cup mint-flavored chocolate pieces for walnuts.

Rocky Road Brownies: Omit walnuts. Fold in ½ cup semi-sweet chocolate pieces, ½ cup chopped peanuts and ½ cup miniature marshmallows.

Apple-Cherry Crisp

The cinnamon-oat topping on this dessert crisps as it bakes. Pictured on page 75.

1 can (21 ounces) cherry pie filling
1 medium baking apple, peeled,
   cored and thinly sliced
2 teaspoons slivered lemon peel
½ cup packed brown sugar
½ cup quick-cooking oats,
   uncooked

¼ cup all-purpose flour
¼ teaspoon ground cinnamon
3 tablespoons butter or margarine
Sweetened whipped cream or
   vanilla ice cream (optional)

1. Lightly grease 10- by 6-inch baking dish. In medium bowl, combine pie filling, apple and peel. Spoon into dish.

2. To make topping: In small bowl, combine sugar, oats, flour and cinnamon. With pastry blender or fork, cut in butter until mixture resembles coarse crumbs; sprinkle over filling mixture. Bake, uncovered, at 375°F. 25 minutes or until golden brown.

3. To serve: Spoon warm crisp into dessert dishes; top with whipped cream or ice cream, if desired. Makes 6 to 8 servings.

GRILLING BASICS

A good barbecue begins with a good fire. And a good fire should become second nature once you've read these few simple tips. First of all, follow your grill manufacturer's directions, whether you're using a gas, electric or charcoal grill.

If you have a charcoal grill, you'll take a couple of extra steps to light the briquettes. To begin, pile them into a pyramid in the center of the firebox. For self-lighting briquettes, simply light them with a long-handled match. For regular briquettes, you'll need to use a liquid, jelly or electric starter. Let liquid or jelly starters soak in at least a minute before lighting. And, to be safe, do not add starter once the first match has been lit or after the fire is going. Let the coals heat until ash gray by day or glowing red after dark.

When the coals are ready, arrange them for indirect or direct cooking. Generally, use indirect cooking for larger cuts that need slower cooking and use direct grilling for thinner, leaner foods that cook quickly. For indirect grilling, arrange the coals around a drip pan and place the food over the pan, so it is not directly heated. For direct grilling, arrange the coals in a single layer and place the food directly above them.

Indirect grilling is the best way to get the smoky flavor of wood, because the food must be covered during cooking. Be sure to add more coals and wood chips to maintain the right temperature, but don't lift the lid more than necessary as it will slow the cooking process. Turn to page 7 for more information on using wood chips.

Grilling food at the right temperature is another key to a good barbecue. Thin foods cook better over hot coals than larger cuts. To judge the coal temperature, hold your hand just above the grid—over the coals for direct heat and over the pan for indirect heat. Then start counting the seconds, "one Open Pit, two Open Pit, three Open Pit." If you need to withdraw your hand after two seconds, the coals are hot; after three seconds, they're medium-hot; after four seconds, they're medium; after five seconds, they're medium-low; and after six seconds, they're low.

The recipes in this book specify direct or indirect heat, coal temperature and whether covering is necessary. All foods were cooked four inches above the coals. Cooking times may vary if these conditions differ.

INDEX